The Music Business Fine Prints

(Everything an artist need, want and should know about the business)

Simone Toussaint, A&R/Artist Developer

Outskirts Press, Inc.
Denver, Colorado

Outskirts Press
http://www.outskirtspress.com

ISBN-10: 1-4327-0581-4
ISBN-13: 978-1-4327-0581-7

Thank You

The steps of a righteous man are ordered by God. I want to begin by thanking The Alpha and Omega for ordering my steps, fore without God I am nothing.

I thank my parents, George and Lenora Toussaint for their un-wavering support, council, guidance, comforting and prayers. To my sister Kathy-Ann, I say thank you for being my sister, I could not ask for anyone better, and even if I could I wouldn't.

I say thanks to my Pastors Peter and Shelly-Ann Bonadie, for their teachings, prayers, and covering.

Last but certainly not least, to Michael Noel, a man with immense talent, skill and vision, for his continued support encouragement, dedication, determination, patience and strength, he constantly kept pushing me to do more than I thought I could do, and for this I say thank you.

I pray that God continue to bless the people who has touched my life and the ones my life has touched.

Contents

Chapter 1
Know the Rules

There is a harsh truth about the music business, and that is people will only help you if they think there is money in it for them, in some cases even loved ones would do the same. The music industry is driven by money, like other successful businesses. I will try to make understanding the music business Simple in this book.

I decided to write based on experiences and other valuable findings within the music industry. This information will help the writers and artists understand the industry beyond just being a singer or writer. **If you don't know the rules, you can't break the rules, if you don't know the game then you can't play,** not unless you like losing, which nobody likes.

I will also give tips on getting your foot in the door, what it entails and how to go about it

To the best of my ability I will try to be specific about royalty percentages earned by artists on record contracts. It is very important to know the numbers you are working with, even though they can change quickly!

Money can be made from DVDs, CD-ROMs, record sales, merchandising, advertising, radio and television.

You might be able to guess which entity generates the real money; it comes from making a record deal. After that a domino effect is created in terms of money. In the United States alone record sales is close to 14 billion dollars annually, Global sales top 40 billion dollars.

No one will spend their resources on an artist who have not created some kind of *buzz* in the industry. Remember if they don't think they'll make money from your art they will not show interest in your art. The real money for a songwriter comes from getting their song on records. Now, if an artist thinks with or without your song they will still make money, then they will not put your song on their record. They have to feel that putting your song on their record will ultimately make them more money. Before we move on let's define who is who, not to get mixed up. An artist, is a person who performs the song. A songwriter, is the person who wrote the song. In some cases the songwriter is also the artist. Gordon Chambers is an artist and songwriter he will make money in different ways, one way is as and artist, performing the song and the other as a songwriter for writing the same song.

Keeping this in remembrance will help you understand the way money is distributed.

As an artist, three important advisors to have is your personal manager, your attorney and your agent, these are the people who will help you make essential music business and career decisions. If you don't trust the person, do not deal with them. It is more likely that you would get a record deal from a reputable record company if your advisors are highly respected. A record company feels more comfortable doing business with an artist who has a personal manager, who happens to be the most important of all the advisors, this is providing you have a good one.

A good personal manager will be responsible for promoting, advising you about what songs to record, who should produce, who to sign contracts with, they coordinate publicity campaigns, cover you from demands that may take up your time such as interviews, and going on tours. The personal involvement of every manager varies.

A personal manager, as compensation, receives between 15% and 20% of the artists *gross* earnings. This is a negotiable percentage. It makes sense to hire a talented personal manager who knows people in the industry and can actively promote you. 20% should not be an issue for such a person, oppose to 15% for someone who cannot help your career. You can negotiate the percentage your personal manager receives for their services after you have become successful and your dollar earnings have grown.

The manager should not be paid from moneys

deposited to an artists account, money that you don't actually keep, for example recording funds that the record company gives artists that is used to pay for studio time or other musicians, and money given for touring.

A personal managers contract has a term period of two to five years; you can have a manager tied to an album release date or just for tour schedules, rather than a fixed weekly or monthly payment regardless to whether or not you have an event, album release or tour scheduled. Your contract with a personal manager should state that she or he is going to be the primary person representing you, not a representative to whom the manager delegates responsibilities. If you don't want to be stuck for a long time with an unproductive managers situation you should include a provision in your contract allowing you to terminate at any time.

Always state the amount of money the personal manager should receive in your contract, for example if you sign a record deal with a record company and soon after you have a disagreement with your manager, you would not want to give 20% of your future profits to him or her and in fact that would be financially upsetting especially since you would have to pay your new manager the same amount from your entire gross income. After the termination of the contract limit the length of time and percentage amount the manager gets.

Because you are into the music business you will want a manager that likes music especially your music, reason being if your manager loves your music he or she will work inevitably harder. You

4

would also want a manager with contacts within the music industry; this will make your process towards getting your foot in the door easier. A manager with too many other responsibilities may not have sufficient time to deal with your business. You should make it a priority to know how many more artists he or she has.

There are very intricate details within the music industry, it will be important to hire an attorney who is knowledgeable about the music business. Attorneys involved in structuring deals artists make would have a vast amount of experience in the field. This knowledge and experience will work in your favor because there are many hidden holes buried in contracts that an attorney who understands the language and numbers would be able to interpret. Understanding what's in your contract is very critical.

It is also important for an artist to understand how your attorney will charge you. Payment may start from $200 an hour and up for a good entertainment lawyer in New York and Los Angeles, other states such as Miami, Atlanta and San Francisco is a little less. If as an artist, it is believed you would definitely be signed to a record label, your lawyer like many lawyers who deal with established artists, will do without a fixed fee and agree to a percentage of the artists earnings it is typically 5%, and this is not to your advantage but theirs.

Like a personal manager you as an artist need to know who your attorney knows in the music industry, it's about who they know and who knows and respect them, also, very importantly are they specialized in music law, if not then you would need to change to an attorney who is in this particular field. Last but not least, who do they represent, in some cases an attorney works for firms that represent both artists and record companies? This may pose a conflict of interest.

Understanding the role of a music agent, they are supposed to book concerts and other appearances for you. When picking an agent allow your personal manager to guide you because your manager and your agent will be dealing with each other most of the time. In some cases, especially in country music, agents are bypassed. Agents agree to be tied to entertainment unions, these unions each have their own form of contracts that agents use with little exceptions.

Agents can charge 10% of an artists gross earnings, only where service was given by the agent. This is one of the exceptions allowed by the unions. In this case the agent will not get income from an artists record sales, songwriting or publishing. The AFM (American Federation of Musicians) and the AFTRA (American Federation of Television and Radio Artists) forms have a place for the artist to initial agreeing to give agent earnings from records; **one should never agree to this.** Some agents would discount the percentage from concerts below the 10% of the artists gross income, especially if the agent wants to have a big name act on board, the fee may be as small as 4% to 5%.

Always try to keep the contract between you the artists and the agent at a one year term limit, doing this will allow you the flexibility to move on if it appears your agent is not performing efficiently to your liking, also, if you bring in major dollars this will allow you to renegotiate for a lower fee.

Before selecting an agent seek the help of your personal manager and attorney with the important negotiating terms. You need to know if your agent is in charge of lining up concerts and appearances, also the territory in which you are represented by your agent. It is important to know the specific duties of your agent in terms of negotiating your engagements. Always consult your attorney to review the terms of your agreement. You will also need a business manager/accountant in addition to your three key advisors. Your business manager/account should be familiar with the shades of expression in the music business. Your business manager/accountant will be responsible for managing your money. Your attorney and personal manager will be able to advise you on choosing a business manager.

Chapter 2
Development Companies

The Entertainment industry continues to grow and change some of these changes are very rapid. The days of submitting a demo on a cassette is no longer seen, soon submitting a demo on CD without a video would be a thing of the past.

Artist development companies are here to rescue new and unsigned artist, they will assist with the developing stages. These companies know what the industry wants and the way in which they will prefer to have thing done. There job is to make sure you are totally ready to be signed to a label and with there inside knowledge they are able to put you on the fast track to a hit track.

Therefore, it is in the best interest of any artist who aspires to become a marking point in this world of entertainment to invest in the knowledge of an artist development company such as themusicip.com, they are affordable, very knowledgeable, with years of experience and consists of management capabilities. In many cases a label will let these development companies know what they are looking for in an artist, this method also protects the label from unsolicited material in addition to getting exactly what they want oppose to listening to thousands of submissions before coming close to what they are looking for. Development companies like themusicip.com work for both the unsigned artist and the label, they save the label time and money, and the artist gets required information which in return saves them time and money also.

Some development companies also manages artist. The difference between management which also boarders on development, and development companies is that, they will work to develop you the way a manager should but won't take 20% of your earnings the way a manager would.

Chapter 3
Record Companies

A record company makes, distributes, and sell records. The record company will also distribute and sell records from other artist, this will normally be done with a distribution agreement. They obtain the right to mechanically reproduce and distribute these records of others acquiring a record agreement with the artist whose music is being recorded.

Record companies vary in size and structure just like publishing companies. There are majors, mini-majors, and independents. Big distribution networks get your records moved from the manufacturing plants and into the record stores where they are sold. The big companies are BMG, UNI, SONY, and WEA. Examples of major labels include RCA Records (BMG), MCA Records (UNI), Columbia

Records (SONY), and Atlantic Records (WEA). The medium-sized companies called mini-majors, which are affiliated with and distribute through one of the bigger companies, and are generally co-owned by one of the majors. They include such labels as La Face Records (Arista/BMG), Maverick Records (Warner Bros/WEA), and Interscope Records (MCA/UNI).

Then there are the major-distributed independent labels. These are created by independent production agreements with established recording artists. These labels include vanity labels like Flip/Interscope (UNI), Big Boy Entertainment/Arista (BMG), Ruffhouse/Columbia (SONY).

This brings us to the small, but true independent record companies that are either self-distributed or distributed through an independent distributor. They have little or no staff, no affiliations with any majors or mini-majors, and are often financed on limited budgets by their owners or investors.

Chapter 4
Your Material

You don't only want to work hard but smart also. At $1.00 + to make and send your demo out, you want it to be effective, that $1.00 should fall in the hand that will make it $5.00+, this will not happen if certain things are not in place, for example you want to have some level of business advisors in place, and you want to create a *buzz*, you want to get the attention of your local community, or any community for that matter.

Because record companies don't want to be the target of a lawsuit they don't accept material they have not requested (unsolicited material). Material sent to a record company will generally not be listened to, even if it's real good.

Because of the volume of CDs and tapes record companies receive it would be difficult to properly listen to them all. The ones that are actually considered are the ones received from a professional manager or attorney who know the major players in the record companies. As the industry grows, major labels are now looking for artists who already have established a history of record sales.

This should not stop you from sending out materials of your work to record companies. Make sure you address your CD or cassette to the Attention of Artist and Repertoire department of the record company. Because image is so important today you can include a photo with your contact information.

Publishing companies make money from owning rights to songs; therefore, the only people who should send material to publishing companies are songwriters. Major publishing companies only offer publishing deals to songwriters when they are certain they can get the artist a record deal or you (artists) agree to have others record your song, especially if they like it. Artists who are songwriters, record deals come first publishing deals come after.

Chapter 5
Internet Distribution

The point about distribution is to place records where it can be purchased. A lot of record labels and artists use the internet to distribute records to fans, many people think distribution dominance will be taken from major label companies due to the massive access to records via the internet. Whereas the internet has its plus side it also poses to be a head ach at times for the artists where piracy is concern.

I don't think the internet takes dominance over the major labels distribution. An artists has to differentiate him or herself from everyone else on the internet, this should be their way of separating the sheep from the goats. The truth is without a record label promoting an artists CD through the many avenues of distribution in media publicity, independent sales breakthrough on the internet will most likely be the exception, not the rule.

If an artists independent sales show to be Promising, whither it be the internet or otherwise, a major label will step in and make an offer to the artists, taking them to the next level.

The record business like any other business does well in good economic times, and not as good in bad times. Record companies will fight over artists and make better deals for the artists in good economic times.

Chapter 6
Record Company Distribution

1. Artist signs a contract with a record company.

2. Artist records the songs in a studio for the record company.

3. The record company makes copies of the master recording

4. The records are shipped to a distributor.

5. The distributor distributes to retailers

6. The record company starts promotion and advertising.

The major label companies are the biggest record companies. The most popular artists are usually represented by major labels, and their name will appear on the CD. An artists record deal will be negotiated with the Business Affairs Department, the most important departments for an artists are the A&R Department, Promotions Department, Marketing Department, and Sales Department.

People in the Artists & Repertoire Department (A&R) are the ones to find new artists and work with them. If an A&R person loves your music and gets you signed with a record label does not mean you would be the next Beyonce.

Being signed is one thing, now one has to be released and sold and in many cases after an artists has worked their way to the signing they're faced with the hard truth, the record company may decide not to release their album!

Most of the people in the A&R department of record companies are not as important in regards to the decision as to which artists gets signed, as some would lead you to believe, in fact, most of the people in the A&R department were hired simply because they have convinced someone in a more influential part of the company that they have an ear that can spot a talented artists.

A chief executive of a major label will hire someone to screen artists, the talented from the not so talented ones (separating the sheep from the goats). Because of the amount of money involve when a new artists is signed, the chief executive and a few key advisors will make the final decisions.

The sales and marketing department work as one. The people in this department take care of promotional merchandise, album-cover artwork, advertising, in-store display and publicity. Although the marketing and sales department deals with some form of promotions there is a promotions department in charge of getting artists records played on the radio. They do a lot of traveling and make friendly conversation with radio station personnel to guarantee your record gets played. The promotional budget can sometimes tell you if a record will be a hit or not.

There are cases where major labels are owned by, or are financially linked to, conglomerates which own the large distributors. The large distributors tend to have more power over record stores than independently owned distributors. There is also the chance of major labels funding smaller labels recording and operating cost in exchange for part of the profit the smaller label may make. There is a very thin line between an independent label that is funded and distributed through a major label and one that is just distributed not funded.

Independent label companies have few, if any, full-time employees. After an artists is signed and their records are recorded with the independent label, the label often, contracts with a major label to deal with the paper work, which includes promotions and marketing. The independent labels would continue to make money if they keep finding talented artists. The difference with an independent label that uses distribution through a major label and a totally independent label is that a true independent label has NO association with a major label.

Choosing a company to sign with is important, simply because you want the BEST representation possible, so you have to ask some questions:

1. Do they like your music?
2. What are their marketing and promotional strategies?
3. What would the level of commitment be, towards your album?
4. Would your record be published even if it appears to be unsuccessful at first?
5. How much money would be spent on your record?

Bigger doesn't always mean better. DO NOT choose a record company just because it is bigger. Most of these companies are bigger because they have a lot of other artists to attend to and in many cases some would be considered more of a priority over others.

Always remember, if the people at the record company like your music and they think it will make them money you would be signed. You would be dropped if you aren't a success right away. This action can make it difficult to get you signed by another major.

Chapter 7
Distributors

Major retailers, will not carry an artists record in store unless the record has a distributor. You want to have your record in as many places as possible. The more places your record can be found the greater the chance of more copies of your record would be sold. This is one of the advantages of being signed with a full staff major label. Some of the major distributors are:

1. Sony Music (distributes Columbia, Epic and Sony)

2. Universal Music Group (distributes Inter scope, Island/Def Jam, and MCA)

3. EMI (distributes Capital and Virgin)

4. BMG (distributes Arista, BMG and RCA

5. WEA (distributes Atlantic, Elektra and Warner Bros.)

These major labels tend to have influential power over the stores and can suggest that the store carry your record. If you decide to use an independent distributor, to sell your CD make sure the distributor is financially sound. Also remember, most contracts between a retailer and distributor are determined by the retailer, they can return any unsold records back to the distributor. A record is in stores between 90-150 days before being returned. Make sure and check your distributor financial statement before signing a contract, that way you can determine based on their financial stance, after the distributor pays salaries and overhead expenses you can be sure to get money also.

In some cases it is better to have a major distributor depending on your style of music, but this is not always the case. Independent distributors may have less power over record stores but more than likely serve your art better than a major. Independent distributors play a significant part in distributing newer styles of underground music, rap and hip-hop; they are also good at getting into the system whereas they can solicit orders more quickly than major distributors.

Jukeboxes use records sold to them from what is called one stop also little retailers who buy in small amount get from one stop. One stop would carry records from many record companies. We also have what is called rack jobbers, they buy records from traditional distributors, then lease space to sell the records in major stores like K-Mart. There is also the case of other consumer access avenues such as Columbia House, BMG Music Services – buy 1get 11 free. These places are licensed by the record companies to sell records to customers.

Chapter 8
Want to Make Money?

Learn to write. It is no secret as to who makes the money in this industry. The writers, the persons married to writers or the artist that has a talented person writing for them. The reason for this as I explained earlier was the fact that these guys get their money before anything else happens to the song.

Whether the song does great or not, really is not the writers problem, in fact it would become the artist problem. Just imagine, I the writer, wrote a song title I ain't FiniSH IT. I get paid for my work and now I can go to my less than humble abode and start writing another song, in the mean time, you the artist was given my song to sing, and if you are a new artist, may God be with you, because at this point you will have to spend a substantial amount of money to make this song (that I the writer wrote and was paid for) not only sound good but also look good to the public, which in return will cause them to buy and you might make some money. Yes I said might make some money. Let me explain, the money you spend to make the song I wrote look and sound good is not your money, it is money loaned to you, and it has to be paid back before you start to make any kind of money.

Let's say the album was a flop two things could happen, the label might keep you for another album in hope that the new one makes enough money to cover both loan expenses or they can drop you entirely.

Now although it's not the artist fault that I ain't finish it was exactly that, the artist who tried their best with the song is the only one leaving the room with empty pockets.

Chapter 9
Payment Calculations

It will be very helpful to you if you have advisors who are versed in the law of entertainment, and very good with numbers, simply because 10% royalty may make you rich or bring you nothing. Therefore understanding royalty payments and calculations is critical, it will help you understand how much money you can make from a record as an artists.

Through distributors a record company may sell a CD at a suggested retail price of $19.98 to a retailer for $13.40. A cut of 10%-14% is taken from the $13.40 by the distributor. The artists royalty rate in most cases is the percentage taken from the suggested retail list price ($19.98), not from the wholesale price received.

Depending on what an artists negotiated their rates will be different, for example; for everyone except successful artists the base rates are reduced by 15% to 20% for sale of CDs, for new artists who has sold under 100,000 albums, royalty rate falls between12% to14% of the suggested retail listed price if the artists is signed to a major, if signed to an independent it's 10% to 14%.

An artist who sells fewer than 500.000 but over 200.000 copies can negotiate a rate of 14% to 16% of the suggested retail list price. A 16% to 18% can be demanded if an artist sell 750,000 copies or more.

A record company will pay a higher percentage to an artist whom they think will generate the sale of records. Whereas an artist may receive 12% on the sale of the first 100,000 units, they may receive 14% on the sale of the next 200,000 units. It is rear for an artist to get over 12% to 14% on a single, far more for new artists, they are not likely to get even 10% of the suggested retail list price.

You need to understand, an artist don't actually get paid on their full royalty rate. Meaning, an artist with a CD royalty rate of 14% of $19.98 which is the suggested retail list price, will not get paid ($2.79) for each CD sold at $19.98, if this was the case, an artist who sell 700,000 copies ($700,000 x $2.79) would generate $1,953,000 in royalties, and this is definitely not the case. Deduction amount and type may vary depending on the form contract of the record company. Always remember to leave room for change. Always review your contract carefully.

Starting with $1,953,000 a deduction for packaging is taken, 10% on vinyl records, 20% on cassettes and 25% on CDs. To calculate CD royalties well start with the suggested retail list price which is: $19.98 minus packaging, which in this case is 25% (25% of $19.98)

$19.98
-4.98
$4.99

So, instead of 14% of $19.98 it will be 14% of $14.99, the artists royalty would be $2.10 per CD. In many cases the artists royalty rate is called all in, this means the artists is responsible for paying their record producers out of their royalties, this leads to another deduction. A producer receives 3% to 4% of the suggested retail list price. Now if the artist pays the producer 4% out of 14%, the artist now remains with 10% of the % $14.99 which is ($1.50). There is a very unusual definition for sold in the record business, an artist receives only 85% of records sold, which boils down to $1.50 on 85 of every 100 records sold, 15 of every 100 records is given to retailers, and for lack of a better word as incentive and irregardless of the reason, it is still 15 CDs given out for free. Reality check, let's say: 700,000 CDs are shipped to the stores,

	700,000.00
Times royalty per CD to the artist	x 1.50
Times royalty bearing percentage	x 85%
Gross royalty to artist	$892,500.00

The record company withholds a part of what is owed to the artist, therefore an artist don't get

$892,500, at least not until the final sale of each record or in the case of returns, after payment is made to the record stores for returned records. An artist should pay particular attention to returns because all of an artists records can be returned if the public is not buying it. Thank God for computer tracking it makes it easy to know which records will come back to the record company. In addition, because of the return privileges, the money the record company holds which is called reserve can be held for two years before the artist is paid.

At least 25% to 40% of the royalties is withheld. A new artist or rock artists, a reserve of 30% to 40% could be withheld, sales generated by new artists are unknown and rock can go cold quickly.

Now from your gross	$892,500.00
Minus 40%	- $357,000.00
	$535,500.00

Note: You may never see the $892,500.00 as an artists far more $535,500.00, because of recoup and advances.

1. Advance – Money paid on an artists behalf, before records are sold.

2. Recoup – Record companies keeps all the money made from record sales.

An artist may never receive royalties from a record company. Also not everything is an advance that is why it is important that the artist negotiates their contract well, it would make sense to have an attorney review the contract before you sign. There are a few other deductions, the biggest ones an artist needs to be aware of are the ones where no royalty payments are made, these are normally on real free goods and promotional copies.

Being in the red, this occurs when the royalties earned by an artist does not cover the amount advanced to them. This amount is carried over to their next record this is called cross-collateralization. Even if their next record is a hit the artist won't see any of their royalties, at least not until the deficit from the first record is paid in full. If the second record does not do well either or there is no second record the record company takes the loss and the artist is no longer responsible for the deficit.

If as an artist you are reviewing proposals from other record companies, compare the dollar amount going into your pocket, not how high the royalty rate is, because sometimes these rates can be misleading.

Note: **Producer royalty payment comes from out of the artists share of royalties. The producer only gets royalties owed after the artist recording cost have been recouped, which by then should be paid immediately.**

It is suggested that an artist insist on having the record company be responsible for paying producer royalties, reason being, if an artists is in the red with the record company from a previous record, the record company will recoup all royalties of the suggested retail list price on the second album, therefore, the record company may not owe the artist a dime after recoup, but the artist will still be owing the producer a whole lot of money.

Chapter 10
Various Royalty Rates

Calculated Producer Royalties

If a producer is working on an album and the budget is $200,000 the advance maybe right around $4,000 per master for each cut. Therefore, 12 songs on an album would give you just about $48,000 per album. A producer can expect an advance of as much as $10,000 per master or more if this is a producer in demand who is working with a large budget. A mixing fee must be paid to the person who does the final mix-down this is whether or not they are also the producer.

A producer now gets a portion of the recording cost in advance from the record company, especially if the producer has his or her own studio.

The money advanced to the producer comes from the advanced to the artist. The advance to the producer can be recouped from artist royalties before the artist gets any money from record sales.

I am sure you've heard the clichés: money is the root of all evil, money can't buy happiness, and so on. Money itself can't be bad it's the pursuit of money that gets people into trouble. Unfortunately record companies are only viewed as the ones who would use anybody to make that money. Record companies exist to make a profit, but so do most companies. Perhaps it's because of the way record companies make their money: they make it from our heroes, the musical artists.

Record companies perform the critical functions that allow artists to reach the masses. This might sound good to you but the problem with the record companies is that they're too gullible and greedy. They sell millions of albums at $15 to $18 an album. Where do the loads of cash go? Does it go to the artist as advance money for marketing and promotional budgets? Where does all that money come from? Who gets what? We will take a look at how record companies work and how the money finds its way from the consumers to everyone who works to get the music to the public.

Record companies locate, finance, and develop new talent; oversee music production; market the music through promotion and advertising and by securing airplay; and distribute the finished product through retail outlets and online services. That is an expensive process considering only about 5 percent of new artists even sell enough records for the record company to break even, and as few as 5 to 10 percent of a labels artists pay for all of the music released by the company.

Before looking at the math behind record deals, a brief disclaimer is in order: the following numbers are generalizations based on a mainstream artist at a major record label. Every negotiated record deal contains different terms and conditions of payment.

Once again, when a label signs an artist, the record company advances the recording budget to the artist at no risk. If the album fails to sell, the artist is not personally responsible for paying the money back. The record company recoups its investment in the album only when the public buys the album. However, the artist does not see any money from the album sales until the label makes back its investment.

A typical recording budget for an artists first album is between $250,000 and $1 million. The record company will also spend approximately $250,000 to $500,000 to market a new artist to the public. Pressing the album and shipping it to retail outlets costs from $1 to $2.25 per unit, depending on the size of the pressing (more units cost less per unit). A new artist typically receives between 12 and 16 percent of the albums suggested retail price as a royalty. In addition to those costs, the record company must pay royalties (called *mechanical royalties*) to the music-publishing company for every unit sold. The record company usually caps its mechanical royalty costs at $0.755 per album (10 songs at $0.0755 per song). To recoup those expenses, the record company receives a wholesale price for each unit sold by the distributor from $7.50 to $11.50 per album, depending on the genre and artist.

With those numbers in mind, we can make some assumptions and show why every record an artist releases is a risky investment for the record company. If the artist receives a $250,000 advance and the record company spends $250,000 on marketing, the record company has spent $500,000 dollars before one album has been sold. If the record company receives $10 per unit from the distributor and has to pay $1.25 for pressing and shipping and $0.75 for mechanical royalties, the record company ends up with $8 per album ($10 income minus $2 pressing, distribution, and mechanical royalties) before deducting the artists royalties. Assuming a suggested retail price of $14.99 and an artist royalty rate of 15 percent, the record company owes the artist approximately $2.25 per unit sold. After deducting the artists royalty, the record company's net income from the sale of the record is approximately $5.75 per unit sold. The record company must then pay for its overhead and all of the albums that don't sell well enough to pay for themselves, $5.75 at a time. For that hypothetical album, the record company must sell 86,957 units to cover its out-of-pocket costs, which do not include the everyday costs of running an international business. Although 86,957 units may not sound like many units to sell, only about 16 percent of all record releases reach that sales figure.

OK it sounds like we have forgotten about the artists, Are they really reaping in the big bucks?

Well, yes and no. Huge stars make lots of money, but most artists, even if moderately successful, generally struggle to make a buck. The artist would not see any royalty money until the record company recoups its advance production budget. The artist usually must pay 3 percent of the royalty to the record producer. Deduct the 3 percent from the royalty rate, and the record company recoups its $500,000 advance at $1.80 per unit sold. Therefore, the artist won't begin seeing money from sales until 277,778 units are sold, and only about 3 percent of records ever reach that sales figure.

You may think the artist could enjoy the advance money he or she received, I'm sure you've heard about the parties artists throw when their big advances come in. Actually, that $250,000 represents a relatively small cost-of-living budget, even if the album sells relatively well. Assuming that no management, attorney, or other professional fees were paid from the recording budget, which would never happen, the artist will probably spend $200,000 of the $250,000 advance on actual recording costs. That leaves $50,000 to split among the rest of members. If it's a band that has five members, each member receives $10,000 to live on until the album recoups its budget, as calculated above. That time period is generally about a year to 18 months if the album sells well.

Furthermore, those calculations don't include the money that the band must pay to its legal team or management for the deal. Lawyers typically charge an hourly rate (from $175 to $350) or a percentage of the artists total gross income (between 3 and 10 percent). Managers typically charge between 15 and 25 percent of their clients gross income. Accordingly, the manager and the lawyer could easily end up with $75,000 of the $250,000.

Artists can earn money from touring, though most bands tour primarily to support album sales and airplay. Also, some artists can make money through endorsements and other marketing strategies. However, the best opportunity for artists to make serious money is to write their own songs.

The primary source of income for artists who write their own songs is mechanical royalties. Typically, a performing songwriter owns his or her own publishing company. That company enters into a co-publishing agreement with a larger publishing company whereby the two companies co-own the copyrights to the songs. Of the mechanical royalty income, the songwriter receives 50 percent, the songwriters publishing company receives 25 percent, and the larger publishing company receives 25 percent.

The publishing company and the songwriter make money from any public performances (for example, airplay and live cover performances) of the albums songs. Although public-performance income is difficult to hypothetically quantify, approximately $0.013 to $0.014 is generated per public performance. That money is divided among the publishing companies and the songwriters. Public performance income is generally not as significant as mechanical royalty income, but if you think about how many times you hear a popular song on a single radio station in a single day and multiply that by the number of similar format stations around the world.

For the songwriter, an album that sells a million copies generates $566,250 in mechanical royalties alone and added income from airplay, which is above and beyond what the band members are making.

That's where the money goes. Hopefully, those figures will help you realistically assess your risks as an artist or songwriter.

Following is a list of other artist royalty rates which are subject to the same previously mentioned deductions.

1. **Budget Records-** These records are sold in stores for less than 60% the royalty rate is 50% of the base rate.

2. **Mid-line Records-** *AKA Catalog item*, this is when the record company is no longer actively promoting a record that has had its run in the initial release. Catalog items are sold to stores at a reduced SRLP of 60% - 80% of a new released top-line record and carry a reduced royalty rate of up to 75% of the artist base rate.

3. **Cutouts and Deletes-** These are records taken out of company catalog because it is dead. An artist receives no royalties on these records.

4. **Coupling and Compilation-** This is when two or more artists appear on the same

album. The royalties gathered by these albums are distributed amongst the artists.

5. **Record Clubs**- Record clubs pay record companies a fee for the privilege to use a recording, this is because the record company has exclusive right to license recordings made for them by an artist. The artist receives royalties of 50% in of their record base rate from record club sales.

6. **Samplers**- These are low-priced albums with a few featured artists. These albums are like coupling, no royalties are paid on them.

7. **Film Soundtrack Album**- Songs leased to film companies by records companies to be used as soundtracks. 50% is usually the artist royalty rate from the record company's licensing fee.

8. **Premiums**- The royalty rate for these records are normally 50% of the base rate. These records are sold with another product attached. Some cereals may carry a musical CD inside. These type of sales should be limited especially if it is being done without the consent of the artist

9. **Foreign Royalties**- Depending on the artist the rates vary extensively. In the United Kingdom, Italy, France, Germany, Japan and Australia the rate is typically 60% to 75% of the base rate, whereas in Canada the typical rate is 85% of the base rate. The Rest of World which is the reference used in

record contracts carries a typical rate of 50% to 60% of the base rate.

10. **Home Video Sales-** This rate comes of the wholesale price of the video and carries a royalty rate of 10%.

11. **Greatest Hits Album-** These rates are based on royalty rates the artist received on the album to which each song initially appeared.

12. **Master Use License-** The record company receives royalties on recordings in advertisement, television, film and internet. These are recordings, licensed to be used. The artist gets paid 50% of the earned money.

13. **Public Performance-** Radio stations in the U.S. do not make payments to record companies for playing their records. Web casters on the other hand must pay! There are many foreign countries that do pay record companies for playing records.

14. **Digital Performance Right-** In some cases the owner of your master recording has a right to receive royalties, the owner could be the record company. New law in 2002 mandates, certain web casters to pay set royalty rates to record companies. An artist should make sure their record contract requires that they receive 50% of the money earned by the record company for any new source of income received by the record company, unless there is a legally specific royalty rate.

Chapter 11
Key Deals

1. **Calculations-** The more records you sell the higher your royalty rate should be.

2. **Contract Options-** Extreme effort should be made to limit the number of consecutive options the record companies insist on receiving.

3. **Record Release-** Release of an album should be guaranteed. Artists need to negotiate this in their contract with the record company. If you are signed with a major label please make sure that your record is released on the record company's main label and not one of their newly found smaller labels.

4. **The Run of the Record-** Always question the commitment of a record company that does not want to commit to a certain dollar amount for the promotion of your record. Proper marketing and promoting determines the life span of your record, without it your record will have a short run and eventually die.

5. **Videos-** If you are with a major label, it would be in your best interest to insist that the label agrees to provide the funds for your video.

6. **On Tour-** Touring can help sell records. At least for your first tour you would want the record company to guarantee full support.

7. **Merchandise Sales-** Make sure your share of the profits in merchandise sales are not used by the record company for loss from record sales. Also you must insist on getting royalty from the sale of merchandise.

8. **Album Artwork-** Remember first impressions last, although your art work can be negotiated, it is not only important that your artwork represent you, it is also important that your artwork is marketable enough to bring in a profit through merchandising.

9. **Multi-media-** Have final control over your art and image, whether in movies or on the web limit the record company's ability to license your work without being approved by you.

10. **Compilation and Coupling-** Have final control over your image do not be forced by record companies to participate in compilation and coupling agreements, this can become very bad for your career in the long run.

11. **Territory-** The record company can sell your record anywhere. If the record company for some reason can not effectively promote and market your album somewhere you may wish to limit their territory.

12. **Reserve-** The time a record company has to hold your reserve should be limited.

13. **Composition Clause-** In record contracts, if the writer and the artist is the same person the money earned is reduced. Understanding how songwriters get paid will also help with understanding the controlled composition clause.

14. **The Masters Ownership-** Whether or not your masters made it on an album you should try to own all of your recorded masters.

15. **Auditing and Accounting-** To avoid constant errors that may go unseen by the record company be sure to have a contract that states you are allowed to conduct detailed audits and periodic accounting that details your record sales, expenses and royalty payments.

16. **Recording Exclusive-** Personal service

contracts consist of Civil Code sections 3423(e) and Code of Civil Procedure sections 526(5). This is for contracts with record companies in California.

Chapter 12
Independent and Major Labels

If an independent label show potential for national distribution, the chances of getting a distribution deal is more than likely to happen. Once an independent label reaches a certain level of success or any smaller label for that matter, the major label record companies has a tendency to buy most of them.

The agreement an independent label signs with a major label to distribute, manufacture, promote and market an already signed independent label artist is called an **Independent Production Agreement.** The major label is required to give the independent label a higher royalty rate than the rate the major label would give an artist, when dealt with directly it is between 2%-5%. The more work the independent label do where marketing and promoting is concern the higher the royalty rate they can expect. Royalty payments to an artist signed to an independent label is the responsibility of the label.

When it comes to profiting through agreements made by both the major and the independent labels, they can either enter into a profit-splitting agreement, this way the work load and profits are split between them. Then there is the independent production agreement which is economically better for an independent label when they have a record that is not as successful, because remember, under the profit-splitting agreement the major label takes on the job of manufacturing and distribution then in return charge the independent label for the cost of everything plus profit, therefore, a moderately successful record under this agreement could leave the independent label with a deficit rather than a surplus.

In some cases an independent label can have a straight distribution deal, this way the independent label will use the major label distribution to distribute records strictly as a wholesaler, which allows the distributor to put a mark up on the wholesale price before selling it to stores. This type of deal can be a gamble for a smaller label simply because they still have to pay all the manufacturing costs, artist royalties, overhead, royalties to songwriters, publishers, marketing and promotion costs and any other cost they may have gathered during the project and whatever is left is profit.

Chapter 13
Songwriters Basic Rules

Songwriters get their money differently from the artist who records the song and this is whether or not the writer is the person recording the song. A songwriter who in many cases is the originator of the song is normally the person who gets the copyrights if the writer is not the originator then its called a work for hire under the U.S., copyright Act which gives a limited duration monopoly to the originator (songwriter) of the song.

Your work has to be of original content and of sufficient materiality before you can obtain the copyright monopoly. In cases such as the May 2006 case with Chris Bridges a.k.a. Ludacris and Kanye West being accused of infringing on a group called I.O.F that did a song titled Straight Like That whereas Ludacris and Kanye did a song titled Stand Up which also used the phrase like that had to be brought before a judge to determine where originality stood based in part on their subject views. This is normally the case when there is a question as to whether or not a song (work) is original. Remember once there is a tangible copy of your work then copyrights exists even if you did not file anything with the government.

After Copyright

The originator (songwriter) after copyright has the right by law to grant exclusive rights to:

1. Reproduce the work
2. Distribute copies
3. Perform publicly

Note: None of the above can be done without the songwriters permission.

When songs (work) as it is called by the Copyright Act is registered with the U.S. Copyright Office the originator (songwriter) can sue for infringement, this is when a songwriter uses a portion of someone else copyrighted song in a new song without permission, when this is done the songwriter can collect the infringers profits.

When the songwriter registers with the U.S Copyrights office they can also collect compulsory license royalties. Work that's joint is written by two or more people. It needs to be made clear if work done on a song was joint-work or not, this protects the writer from someone claiming that their contribution to the work was intended as joint-work. As for arrangements of songs there is hardly any copyrightable protection. The arrangement must be original and of sufficient identifiable material, it can not be just an expression of an idea. A song produced in a studio where the producer help by adding key instrumental tracks towards bringing out the desired song does not entitle them to a copyrightable interest. Songs written by someone for someone else either as an employee or independent contractor is known as work-for-hire.

Copyright Exceptions

1. If the song is a non-dramatic musical composition.
2. If the song was previously recorded and distributed publicly in phonorecords with the copyright owners permission.
3. If the requested license is for the use of your song in phonorecords only.

The license must be granted by the copyright owner if the above list is true when it involves the use of a song on a record, this is one of the important exceptions under the Copyright Act to a songwriters exclusive monopoly rights.

A song first published legally in the U.S., does not need any copyright notice on or after March 1, 1989, but giving notice could help in court if someone should infringe on your work. A person can use © symbols but to be able to collect license royalties or sue for infringement, a copyright must also be registered with the Copyright Office.

Getting your songs heard

It is best to have a music attorney or someone in

the business end send out your songs, because people in the business are afraid of frivolous lawsuits to which they are a target, especially when people claim that their songs were stolen. Your song has more credibility when it is initially dealt with by someone in the business end of the music industry.

Income Sources

Primary sources of income are:

1. Royalties paid by the record company. Also known as mechanical royalties.
2. Payments by television stations, radio stations, restaurants and others for playing the song publicly is known as performing royalties.

Mechanical royalties are normally paid by the record company to the copyright owner of a song. Payment is negotiated between the record company and the copyright owner. A song written, owned or controlled, in whole or in part by the artist is known as a controlled composition.

The performance rights society in the U.S., ASCAP and BMI are the dominant performance rights societies. Before they came into existence every nightclub, restaurant, and other places that played music publicly was charged a fee, which can get really crazy.

BMI songs played on commercial radio generate at least 6 cents per play. Songs reaching number 1 on the Billboards Hot 100, is more than likely to be played enough times to generate $250,000 to $500,000 in performing royalties. A songwriter will need to collect from the publisher shares from performing royalties, providing that they are entitled.

Foreign mechanical and performing rights is another form of income for songwriters, as for well-known songs attached to commercials, can earn from $50,000 to over $1,000,000, this is possible through a synchronization (sync) license which is issued to companies, such as those producing television shows, movies and anything of this nature. Sheet music containing a single song is paid by a sheet music company and is typically 20% of the retail selling price.

Chapter 14
Publishing and Publishers

First things first, holding on to your publishing is a big deal and that's because if you are with a good full service publishing company they will find everybody and anybody who can use your songs, to use your songs and then negotiate licenses with the users. They will make sure that royalties are paid, that public usage is reported so that performing royalties are not lost, and this report is made to the **Performing Rights Society.** You see a good publisher will make you a lot of *good* money.

Note: Do not enter into a contract with a publisher if you don't believe they will make you money.

There are deals that can be established between writer and publisher, one is a co-publishing deal, and this is where the songwriter and a publisher agree to share the publishing. The other is an administration deal, where there are no advances and the administrative task of the publishing company is limited.

Chapter 15
Contract Deal Points

Terms: This is usually for one year between songwriter and a major publisher. In terms of a writer artist development deal this may be for as long as two years.

Rights: Transferred: There are some exercises you may not want your publisher to perform without your approval, like Changing the words or music of your song, changing the title, synchronizing to X-rated films or advertisements, allowing someone else to change your song and share in the royalties, or translate into a foreign language.

Royalties: Even if you are entitled to receive part of the publishing make sure that the publisher you are dealing with can not issue mechanical licenses at less than the usual rate to its affiliates.

Advances: This is an advanced amount given to the signed songwriter based on how much money the publishing company expects to make from the songs, advances will be recoupable from royalties when received.

Limitations: The publishers are paid quarterly by the record company and even though this is the case, publishers try to pay songwriters twice a year. The songwriter should try by any means necessary to get their publisher to pay them quarterly.

Reversion: It is the songwriters responsibility to seek his or her own best interest; this is why when the rights to your songs are sold to the publisher for the life of the copyrights in exchange for royalty payment participation, you should negotiate for reversion of copyrights if certain duties are not met by the publisher within a reasonable time period.

Work for Hire: A work for hire is when a person creates a copyrightable work but does not own it. The Copyright Act allows for the copyright to go not to the creator but to the person who hired the creator to make the work. The law ignores the contribution of the creator of the work and focuses on the employer who owns the copyright and treats it as if the employer created the work themselves without any help from the actual creator.

Musicians should be very careful of work for hire contracts. Under a work for hire contract, you have absolutely no right in the music you create. In the case of commercials, you will have to sign a work for hire contract. The company who makes the product will want the rights to the jingle you create.

If you sign a work for hire contract to play with a band, you will not be entitled to any royalties or even credit for your work other than what the band agrees to pay you. It will be as if you never existed and the band will be considered the creator of your music.

A work for hire is not the same thing as transferring ownership in a copyrightable work. You may create a song and then sell it to a company for a commercial. This is not the same thing as a work for hire.

You have more rights if you create a song yourself then transfer it than if you had a work for hire contract. The Copyright Act allows an author of a song to get it back even after transferring. If you transfer a song to someone, you may serve written notice on the person who holds the copyright between the thirty-fifth and fortieth years after transferring the copyright and get your song back! A work for hire contract is something you should try to avoid. Fortunately, there are specific criteria needed to create a work for hire. A copyrightable work will be considered a work for hire if you are an employee and create the work in the course of your employment. If you see a contract that has the words work for hire in them, you should pay very close attention to it. Be careful with these types of arrangements.

Minimum Songs: The songwriter is required to have an average of twelve songs per year. If it was collaboration (A song done by you and someone else) the writer receives credit for half the song. Be sure that you are not prohibited from collaborating with different song writers irregardless to whom their publishers might be.

Exclusive: As songwriters make sure you have some flexibility in certain situations even though your agreement may be exclusive with the publisher, like in the case of writing a song for film, the film company will insist on receiving the copyrights.

Co-Publishing: A co-publishing deal is entered into when two publishing companies are publishers of a song, like when songwriters collaborates on a song and have different publishers. It is always better to keep your administration or have your publishing company keep it, this will deal with the question as to who is entitled to administer the song and get paid for it.

Infringement: Sorry I can't say infringement claims comes cheaper by the dozen, in fact when someone claims that you infringed on their song it can start a costly up hill battle legally. You should insist at the very least that if the lawsuit is unsuccessful that the publisher will pay for its share of the legal fees. Be aware that the publishing company will insist on being compensated for the full cost of the lawsuit, keeping control over the litigation, and instead of paying you, they'll hold as a reserve the money being sued for, and it does not matter if the lawsuit is true or not.

Foreign Sub-publisher: In many cases a sub-publisher is used to collect royalties from other countries. As a songwriter you want to share royalties 50/50 with your publisher before the sub-publishers share is deducted, this is so that you don't pay publishing twice.

Auditing and Accounting: Nobody can seek your best interest better than you, therefore, when it comes to your money you want to be hands on and in the face of every aspect of it. Your contract should allow you to have a detailed audit of the publishers books; periodic accounting from the publishing company should be done, covering payments received by the record companies, licensing fees received for use of songs, payments from sub-publishers and any expense charged to your account.

Note: Before the song has been recorded and distributed publicly with the copyright owners permission a compulsory mechanical license need not be given. Also for the exception of performing rights monies paid directly to the songwriter from ASCAP or BMI the songwriter should receive 50% of all monies collected by the publisher.

Your Own Publishing Company: First you want to apply with the performing rights society, this is so that you can be clear of having a name similar to another company, because if that's the case BMI/ASCAP will not collect money for you, (they will turn your application down). If you are a songwriter and a publisher you must apply separately to the same performance right society. You will be provided with a list of BMI and ASCAPs affiliates.

In most states you must file a document with the county recorder if your company is not a corporation using a corporate name. Depending on which state you're in the name of the document may vary but your county recorder should be able to guide you. You need to register your songs with the US Copyrights Office in Washington D.C.

Chapter 16
Sampling

This is a serious subject; it is the practice of copying or transferring snippets or portions of a preexisting copyrighted record to make a new body of work. An artist will take a piece of a pre-existing recording and use it to create a new recording. Basically sampling is not original works of a previous copyrighted song. The right to prepare non original works based on copyrighted works is one of the rights of the copyright owner. As such, the copyright owner must grant permission before the copyrighted song(s) can be used.

Fair Use
It has been said that sampling only three notes is not copyright infringement because it is protected as

fair use. If you sample a single note, beat, or line from a sound recording without permission, establishes copyright infringement. Under US copyright law, unauthorized sampling - no matter how minimal or seemingly harmless- is usually not considered fair use. Copyright infringement is not the number of notes sampled, but whether the sample is similar to the original work. The other question is whether it should qualify as fair use. Contrary to popular belief and practice, sampling of an original copyrighted song without the owners permission is illegal copyright infringement.

If you sample without permission, not only are you transgressed against the US Copyright laws, you would more than likely also be in violation of your own recording contract. Most recording contracts contain several provisions called Warranties, Representations and Indemnification, this is a promise from you to the label that all the material on your album is original and you agree that if your label is sued for copyright infringement, you will reimburse them for all their court costs, legal expenses and attorneys fees.

There are warranties and indemnification clauses which exist in the distribution agreements between your record company and the retail stores. Therefore, when you violate copyrights law by sampling without proper permission, everything points back to you as the artist. Further more, it is very costly when you sample illegally which generally ranges from $500 to $20,000 for a single act of copyright infringement, you can be liable for damages up to $100,000 if the copyright owner proves you willfully encroach on their work. The infringer is also forced to recall all the illegal copies of the song in the albums and destroy them this is called the destruction procedure. You may even face criminal charges from the U.S. Attorneys Office.

Chapter 17
Artist Royalties

This amount is a paid percentage of the suggested retail list price of the record less deductions. License fees from film/TV, CD-ROM/DVD, advertisement, and the internet is paid to the artist by the record company as agreed in the record contract.

Chapter 18
Songwriter Royalties

In mechanical royalties the publisher pays the songwriter from record sales received from the record company for the right to include his or her songs on a record. From the 100% the publisher receives in royalty payments 50% goes to the songwriter. In the case of performing royalties from airplay paid by radio stations, television stations web broadcasters and other public performances the royalties is also divided into two equal parts 50% is the writers share and 50% is the publishers share. This payment is made directly from the performance rights society to the songwriter. Another way in which the songwriter makes money is from sheet music sales, film/TV, advertisement, internet and CD-ROM/DVD sync license fees, which is paid in the same form as mechanical royalties.

Chapter 19
Your Own Publishing Company

Publishing rights are the rights to a song. If you write a song by yourself, you own the publishing and copyright. You don't have to own a publishing company to own the rights, which is automatically with authorship.

The publishing dollar is almost always split in two parts, one of the halves is called the Writers Share, the other half is called the Publishers Share and you own that half as well, unless you sign a publishing or co-publishing deal. You can give up some of the publishing rights you own in exchange for a cash advance from a music publisher. The publisher will then work towards getting your song cut by an artist or placed in a movie or TV show. They don't make money unless they get the song used.

If you are one of those people who is thinking about starting your own publishing company, take note, people typically start a publishing company when they get a song cut and need a mechanism or company to which they can have the income flow. One word of advice, it's often a better idea to have another company administer your publishing when you have your own publishing company. They will take care of all the business of collecting and distributing the money that is generated by the song. Many small or individual publishers don't have enough experience to do this alone.

A song generates money for the writer(s) when it appears on an album, gets played on the radio, used in a TV show or movies, gets sold as sheet music, and even when it is used as a ring tone on a cell phone. When the song is part of an album or is sold as sheet music, the writer gets a mechanical royalty. When a song is used in a movie or TV show, a performance royalty is paid to the writer(s).

Chapter 20
Publishing Contracts

Exclusive Song Writer Agreement: Also known as staff writer contract, the song writer generally grants the publishers entire share of the income to the music publisher. The writers services are exclusive to the music publishers for a period of time. Therefore, any compositions written within that period belongs to the music publisher. These deals are usually offered to writers with who has some level of success. If the writer has a track record of writing hits, the publisher in return is confident that they will recoup from the initial investment. In return for signing exclusive rights to some or all of the writers songs, the writer gets paid by the publisher a negotiated advance against future royalties. The advance amount naturally depends on the writers bargaining power and on the competition in marketplace.

Single Song Agreement: A single song agreement is a deal between the writer and the music publisher in which the writer grants certain rights to a publisher for one or more songs. In single song agreements, the writer is paid a one-time recoupable advance.

Co-publishing Agreement: The most common deals are co-publishing agreements. Under this deal, the songwriter and the music publisher are co-owners of the copyrights in the musical compositions. The writer becomes the co-publisher with the music publisher based on an agreement in regards to the royalties and how it would be split. The song writer assigns an agreed percentage to the publisher, sometimes. A 50/50 split, the writer conveys ½ of the publishers share to the publisher, but retains writers entire share. In a typical 75/25 co-pub deal, the writer gets 100% of the song writers share, and 50% of the publishers share, or 75% of the entire copyrights, with the remaining 25% going to the publisher. Thus, when royalties are due and payable, the writer/co-publisher will receive 75% of the income, while the publisher will retain 25%.

Administration Agreement: An administrative agreement takes place between a songwriter/publisher and an independent administrator, or between a writer/publisher and another music publisher. In an admin agreement the songwriter self-publishes and licenses songs to the music publisher for a term of years and for an agreed royalty split. Under this agreement, the music publisher simply administers and exploits the copyrights for another publisher/copyright owner. Only the most well known song writers can even consider asking for an admin deal. Under this coveted arrangement, ownership of the copyright is usually not transferred to the administrator. Instead, the music publisher gets 10-20% of the gross royalties received from administering.

Collection Agreement: A collection agreement is like an admin deal where the writer retains the copyrights, the difference is that the publisher does not perform exploitation functions; like a business manager, it merely collects and disburses available royalty income.

Sub-publishing Agreement: These are basically music publishing deals in foreign territories between a US publisher and a publisher in a foreign territory. They are like admin or collection deals with no ownership of the copyrights being transferred to the sub-publisher, but limited to one or more countries outside the US. Under this publishing deal, the publisher allows the sub-publisher to act on its behalf in certain foreign territories.

Purchase Agreement: Under this agreement, one music publisher acquires in whole or in part the catalogues of another music publisher, similar to a merger of companies. In this case, an investigation is done to determine the value of the catalogue.

Chapter 21
Building the Band

- The first thing is to get a set together of at least 10 songs. This can be covers or your own original material.

- Next, get practice. Develop your performance skills. Join the pub circuit. Perform in school concerts, at weddings or wherever you can. The important thing is to learn to work with an audience and fine tune your set.

- If your aim is to become professional, join the Musicians Union. The Musicians Union has lots of information which gives advice on turning professional.

- Find a manager. If a member of your band is interested in this then they might be able to fill this role. They will need to negotiate venues, rates and contracts.
- The managers role is to ensure the band builds up a profile. If the band wants a record deal the managers role is also to make sure that the right people come to the gigs.
- The manager will also be responsible for negotiating record deals and TV appearances.
- If you sign a record deal it is also important to copyright your material. There are a number of ways of doing this. The Performing Rights Society will be able to give advice on this.

Chapter 22
Issues, Issues and More Issues

One of the main issues with bands is **money** especially when they no longer like each other or just don't get along, therefore, you want to be in a band with people you know, respect and like. This is mainly because you not only have to be with each other all the time; you would also be doing business together. In the beginning you may not see all that can go wrong while being in a band but just to be on the safe side you should have an internal band contract, either in the form of a Limited Liability Company, a partnership or corporation; this should be done especially if you think the band is going places. The internal contract should include issues such as; who owns the bands name in the event of a break-up? How are artistic decisions made if there is a disagreement? Who gets what percentage in profit? What would happen to a former members interest if he or she quits or is fired? Who controls business decisions? Who owns the song writing and publishing interest? This might be the most critical of questions. The band members need to be clear on the issues of whether or not the band owns the copyrights or just one person and what happens to the copyrights if the band breaks-up? These questions should be dealt with before hand, this way you would know where everybody stands, and waiting until the band is signed to a major label just might be too late to address these issues.

Develop a Strong Teams and Partnership by:

1. Finding someone whose strengths complement your weaknesses and set up a trial period to see if you can work well together.
2. Define who will contribute the cash, property, or expertise.
3. Communicate regularly to avoid power grabs and misunderstandings. Talk openly, honestly and relentlessly with your partners.
4. Specify the percentage of ownership each person will have and define how, when, and in what order the profits will be distributed to partners.
5. Prepare a business plan and financial expectations for the life of the partnership.
6. Provide a way to remove or buy out partners who fail to meet their obligations. Shit happens.

7. Prepare for this beforehand and you'll save countless hours of heartache and stress later.

Chapter 23
Music & Movies

Music in the movies is one of the main factors that help to determine box office success or failure. You may begin to realize the value and contribution of music and lyrics to film if you could visualize a motion picture without any lyrical content.

Most feature films are produced either by the major Hollywood studios or by U.S. and foreign independent production companies. Filmmaking costs has gone through the roof in recent years. The average cost to produce market and advertise a film today is in excess of $75 million. Films are now financed in a variety of ways including major studio backing, joint ventures, outside private or public investors, among others. The investing parties involved normally have a good idea of the revenue-producing areas from which their investment will be recouped.

There are thousands of films produced each year worldwide which do really well, and make lots of money which in return create income opportunities for composers and songwriters.

A film producer who wants to use a song in a motion picture must get the permission of the music publisher. Once a fee agreement is reached, the producer will sign what is known as a synchronization or broad rights license, which will give the studio the right to sell it to television, use the song in motion picture theater trailers or television and radio promos, and sell videos. The synchronization fee received by the music publisher is shared by contract with the songwriter The synchronization fees charged by music publishers for major studio films are usually between $15,000 and $60,000 (with the majority ranging from $20,000 to $45,000) but can be lower or higher depending on how much times the song is used, when it is used whether it's in the opening or closing credits and last but not least if it of extreme vital importance to a specific scene or plot. The same song may be licensed at very different rates for different projects. I should also inform you that record companies normally charge between $15,000 and $70,000 for the use of existing master recordings in a major studio film. If a producer uses a song more than once in a motion picture, the fees charged by music publishers will obviously be higher than if the song is only used once.

Sometimes a film producer will request

permission for a change in lyrics to the song which will either be re-recorded for the film or sung by one of the characters in the in the film. When such a request is received, a music publisher should ask for a copy of the new lyrics, a plot summary of the film, and a scene description including script pages so that it knows exactly how the song will be used before making a decision. When a successful recording artist on a major label records the song for the film guarantees of an A side single release is sometimes made. In this case, the publisher may give two price quotes; a higher figure if the song does not make the soundtrack album or if an album is not released. For example, if a publisher gives a $24,000 quote for the use of a song in a film, it also might agree to reduce the price to $21,000 if there is a guarantee of a nationally distributed soundtrack album and may even further reduce the fee if the song becomes an A side single from the album.

When a producer hires a composer or lyricist to write a song for a film, the contracts typically state that the producer employs the composer or lyricist to write a song within a stated period of time with certain ideas and instructions given by the producer. When the song is delivered, the writer receives an initial fee (for example, $25,000 for a song; $2,500 for the lyrics) as well as a guarantee of additional future compensation in the form of songwriter royalties which are contained either in the body of the agreement or attached as a separate schedule (i.e. 50 percent of mechanical income earned from record, tape and CD sales; a set rate for sheet music; 50 percent of any synchronization income from the uses of the song in a television series, other motion pictures, or advertising commercials, etc.). The writer also normally receives screen credit for the composition, for the writing fee, the writer usually grants all rights to the producer under an employee-for-hire or work-for-hire contract.

The writing fee will be negotiated depending upon whether lyrics, music or both are being contracted for as well as whether a producer and artist is involved. Some of the main considerations as to the amount of the fee are the nature of the production. The past success of the writers, the music budget, the type of use and the experience and influence of an agent involved. Fees can range from below $1,000 to over $100,000 for a song with additional monies due for a master recording.

If the writer is a record producer or an artist, the fees will normally be separated according to the different aspects of the services. The song will normally be specified as a work for hire with practically all rights and publishing owned by the Producer. Most major studios and production companies own their own publishing companies and assign the film songs to these entities.

Some major writers are able to negotiate retention of all music publishing or a co-publishing deal with the studio or Production Company but this is the exception rather than the norm. Also, some writers are able to get the song back from the studio if the song is not used in the picture, but again, this is a matter of negotiation.

The composing fees paid to a feature film composer vary considerably depending on the past success and stature of the composer; the amount of music needed in the film; the type of music required; the total budget for the film; the total music budget, including the cost for licensing preexisting outside songs or master recordings; whether the film producer is a major studio, a major independent, or a minor player in the film world; the size of the orchestra needed to record the score; whether the composer is contracting to bear all or most of the costs of music or only negotiating the composing fee; whether the film is intended for wide distribution or only a limited release; the standard fees paid by a particular studio versus the fees of other studios; and the skills of the individuals on both sides of the negotiation fence-- the studio and the composers agent. Depending on many of the above factors, composing fees can range from $20,000 for a lower-budget film to in excess of $1,000,000 for a big-budget studio release using the services of a well-known composer.

The primary composer royalties, in addition to the composing and services fee contained in most background composer contracts include all or most of the royalties as set forth in the standard songwriter agreement including the right to receive performance royalties, mechanical royalties, sheet music and folio royalties, foreign royalties and synchronization royalties, among others. If the composer is also the producer of the soundtrack album as well as the conductor on the album, additional producer and artist royalties will be negotiated. For example, a sample clause might provide 3% of the suggested retail price of a CD

(6% wholesale) as a producer and 7% of retail (14% of wholesale) as a conductor with a pro-ration based upon the number of other outside tracks on the CD.

Scoring a film or having a song in a film can provide a lifetime of earnings to a composer or songwriter. In addition to the initial writing or synchronization fee, composers and songwriters can earn royalties from many sources including record, CD and tape sales, U.S. and foreign television, cable and radio performances, theater performances, downloads, streaming and artist and record producer royalties, among others. In order to make sure you receive what you are due, you must know what is in the contracts you are signing, the many considerations involved, and the areas that are open for negotiation as well as those that are standard for everyone. Writing for film involves creativity but it also involves a multi-billion dollar worldwide business. Knowledge of how the business works is essential for success in this area.

Chapter 24
The A&R

The record label A&R position is probably one of the most hectic jobs in the music business. A&R stands for Artists & Repertoire. The main function of a record label A&R is to help their artists creatively while helping the record company financially by signing hit acts and developing them. They are usually music industry professionals that are hired to oversee the entire recording process which includes finding the right songs for their artist, working with the right music producers, and finding the right recording studio, a major record label A&R must stay on top of current music industry trends in order to create acts that will do well for the record label that employs them. Even if a record company A&R really likes a band they still may not be able to sign them. Usually it is the head record label A&R that makes the final decisions. The reason why being an A&R can be extremely stressful is because with every act that you sign your job is on the line. Since there is a high rate of failure in the music industry A&R people try to sign artists that are already somewhat established. If an A&R does not prove to the record label that they can generate hit acts, their services will be terminated.

A&R people were producers, promoters or artists themselves. Record company A&R people are in their thirties because they are old enough to know what they are doing & young enough to know what the new trend is. Its only the beginning when you get signed. Your record label A&R person may have to deal with flaky or unhappy music producers that aren't really into the project and are too busy to put their heart in it. Your A&R must also fight for you to get the attention of the record labels publicity, sales and promotion departments. It definitely takes a lot of work on an A&R person's part to get a recording artist from signing to being added to radio play lists and having a video on MTV. The recording process for a record label A&R is very intense because they must make sure that there are enough radio friendly songs on the release. If the A&R feels like there are not enough quality songs he / she will have the artist write and record more.

The labels that accept unsolicited material may ask you to put a certain code on your package so that they know you have permission to submit.

Most A&RS know exactly what they are looking for in an artist and if they see it in you they will more than likely sign you without any hesitation. If you market and promote yourself aggressively there is a chance that a record label A&R will come to you. Chamillionair did not need to be signed he become a local hit and sell a good amount of CDs on his own, next thing that you know a majority of the major record labels wanted to sign them.

Record companies these days spend less time developing acts. Your package should include 3 of your greatest songs with the best one first because most A&R people will not keep listening unless the first song gets their attention. Sometimes an artist will send in a full complete CD with out a note telling the A&R which song or songs they should listen to, most don't have time to listen to the whole CD and didn't feel like searching around for a great song. In the package you must also include a quality 8x10 photo, a biography that tells the A&R a story about the artist and how much local or regional success he / she has. Make sure that you leave your contact information home address, email address, home phone cell phone, etc. Make sure that your demo CD is clearly and neatly labeled.

Chapter 25
Getting Your Music Where It Belongs

Since managers, producers & publishers act as filters for the A&R people you may want to get them to shop your demo for you. Your demo may have a better chance of someone listening to it if the person who sends it is well known or has a track record in the music industry. You can use music industry resource to find a successful music manager, producer or publisher to shop your music. This music business is all about being professional and persistent, I suggest you work hard at getting your music to the people who can make things happen. A&R people hate when representatives call them or leave messages that are full of *hype* the only thing this does is make them never want to meet you.

The internet is becoming a great way for people to find new talent because artists are becoming savvy enough to get sites up with MP3 samples of their music. Technology is making the job of finding new talent easier and easier. There are a lot of magazines out there that offer demo reviews for artists, like music connection magazine.

An Artist and Repertoires job is to research potentially profitable artists. They tend to like artists that are already selling albums locally and are having those records counted by sound scan. An A&R looks for:

1. Hit songs.

2. Star quality front person that looks good, has style and charisma.

3. Has a great powerful stage presence and performance. Let's face it sex sells and will sell until the end of humanity. Some artist need to get makeovers before they could be seen as a star quality recording artists.

Chapter 26
Solicited Work

When a record label A&R, music manager, music publisher or music producer states that they only accept solicited material this basically means that you need to ask permission to send a package. Simply mailing them your demo and promotional material in high hopes that they will listen to your music is not likely to be successful, although this strategy has worked for some artists in the past. Making contact with your intended music industry professional and making sure that they are expecting your package seriously increases your chances of being heard. It is also important to get your songs mastered by a professional before sending them out. You should definitely make contact with those that accept unsolicited material to make sure that they are expecting your package as well. You should always call first before submitting your material. This will ensure that your package will get priority over another unsolicited package.

You don't have to be a famous music mogul to be solicited. When speaking with A&RS, managers, publishers and producers you must be extremely professional even when you are speaking with an assistant. These people are responsible for filtering out calls from amateurs. **The important thing is to build a relationship with everyone you come in contact with.** Find out the names of everyone that you come in contact with. Ask them questions like who they have worked with in the past and what styles of music they prefer. It is much better to pinpoint A&RS, Managers, producers & publishers that work in your style of music. Don't waste your efforts! Always be ready to explain who you are and what you are doing.

If you have a website with some music clips the manager or label will tend to listen to what you have to say. Don't ever call a record label like a JC (just come). These days the most important thing an artist can have is a website. When calling record labels it is extremely important to make friends with assistants, secretaries & receptionists. Ask them if they will accept your package and listen to your music. You may even be doing them a favor by entertaining them for a few minutes. Remember that some people who work at record labels are just doing a job and sometimes don't get the money or respect that they deserve. Try and light up their day with your upbeat personality. If you want to be in the music industry you must be able to handle rejection as well.

Negative results should make you more persistent and determined to prove to them that you are important. Don't be surprised if people are rude or a little hard to deal with, this is the music business. You may have to kill them with kindness. At least if they hear your name and listen to your music you made a new contact in the music industry. When an assistant answers the phone you should already know what you are going to say to him or her. Don't sound anxious or be overly aggressive. Think of the assistants, receptionists and secretaries as a filter.

The warning no unsolicited material is usually used so that record companies don't get swamped with submissions. It's not that A&RS and Managers don't want to listen to new material. It's more like they don't have the time to listen to everything. If a record label hasn't heard of you yet you should always give them a call first. When your package is solicited it gets priority over something that is not solicited. This doesn't necessarily mean that they aren't going to listen to your music at all. Most record labels do have people that listen to unsolicited material. It is usually an assistant A&R or an intern. Other companies may throw unsolicited material away or send it back to you. Music history has shown that a lot of huge artists where discovered by someone listening to unsolicited material.

Record Labels, music managers, music

publishers and music producers get a good number of packages each day. When you call them to let them know that you are going to send a package, ask them for some kind of code that you can write on the package so that they know it is solicited. This is not necessarily standard practice by most labels anymore but they will still do it. **Another great way to ensure that your package will get reviewed is to have a messenger deliver it.** I know it is expensive so only use this tactic when your odds are good. Only use this strategy when your intended target is looking for an artist or producer with your characteristics.

Information from BMI and ASCAP has reported collecting over $638 million dollars in performance royalties in 1992. First, the two groups take all the revenue and pay their expenses. This is done by dividing the money up between all their members. Both ASCAP and BMI keep track of what music is played and how frequently. Radio stations must keep log books reporting every song they play. BMI and ASCAP then compile all these reports and apportion the revenue they collect among the songs which were performed publicly. In this way, a Top 40 song which is played every 2 hours will get more performance royalties than a song which is only played once a week.

To join BMI, call (212) 586-2000 and to join ASCAP, call (212) 621-6000. Ask for a writer application packet. Both organizations represent music publishers as well, but that is beyond the scope of this column. The fee for a writer to affiliate with ASCAP is $10 while there is no fee

for writer affiliation with BMI. Finally, you can only join one organization since they both require an exclusive agreement with a songwriter.

Touring

This is done primarily to promote record sales. Some of the important matters in a tour agreement include merchandizing, limiting promoter expense, and technical specifications. (Lighting, stage setup etc).

Before you as an artist set out for tours make sure you have a written contract signed by the club owner before you show up. If you are a new artist it is advised that touring for you should wait until your record is out. Although it takes a lot of money to be on tour, a major star will make money.

Chapter 27
Merchandise

Until you are a major star you may not make much money from merchandise sales. You would have to take into consideration that there are rules once you start selling. You have city taxes, sales taxes, business license fees and local fees that must be paid and since more than likely you would not be doing the selling alone, you may have a friend help you, now you have payroll taxes and in some cases worker compensation.

Chapter 28
Internet

It is extremely difficult to determine the appropriate fee that should be paid for use of a song via the internet. Therefore it is the responsibility of the song writer to make sure your publishing deal calls for you, as the songwriter to receive the full songwriters share of income generated from the internet.

Chapter 29
Video Games

In recent years, the Video game industry has been the fastest growing area of the entertainment business. Music is a major part of many of these games. For songwriters, recording artists, film and television composers, music publishers and record companies, the video game industry represents a new and valuable source of income.

With regards to re-existing songs, there are a number of different ways to license music in this area depending on the success of the song being used, the type of video game, how the game is distributed and the policies of the manufacturer. Some agreements provide for an actual royalty but many provide for a one-time buy-out fee per composition regardless of the number of games actually sold or how many times the game is played. The percentage per game royalty ranges from 8 cents to 15 cents per composition and buyouts range from $2,500 to over $20,000. Royalties and fees depend upon the value of the composition, the prior history or anticipated sales of the game, bargaining power of the parties and the needs of the video game producer, music publisher and songwriter.

Some agreements have a set term, during which the song can be used in the video game. If there is a set term, the video manufacturer will many times have the right to sell off its inventory of games for a period of time once the term is over. Other licenses last for as long as the video game is in distribution. Many game producers receive the right to release the compositions used in the video game in companion products such as an audio CD or separate DVD release of the game. Sometimes fees are actually set in the agreement and other times there is a good faith negotiation provision as to the ultimate fee that will be charged.

Chapter 30
Foreign Royalties

There are societies similar to ASCAP around the world, and we cooperate with them to ensure that our members receive royalties from performances of their works abroad. ASCAP has agreements with foreign societies representing virtually every country that has laws protecting copyright. We license the works of their members in the U.S., and they license the works of our members in their territories.

ASCAP is the most effective U.S. performing rights organization in collecting foreign royalties. ASCAP has the longest-standing relationships with foreign societies; they have the deepest understanding of how they do business. ASCAP aggressively monitors foreign performances of

ASCAP works in all media to ensure that our members are being paid correctly. ASCAP is the only society to have an International Monitoring Unit that utilizes an innovative database (EZ-MAXX) to verify the accuracy of television performance statements received from affiliated foreign societies.

There revenues from foreign territories have steadily increased as the result of their efforts and the growing prominence of American music abroad. they also want their members to receive money from abroad as quickly as possible, which is why ASCAP make four foreign distributions - in February, May, August, and November - in any given tax year. ASCAP members also have a unique opportunity to take advantage of a foreign tax credit as a result of enhanced year-end reporting of earnings. ASCAP has a full-service membership office in London that provides a wealth of functions for ASCAP members who live, travel or has business abroad. ASCAP also plays a prominent role in CISAC, which is the international confederation of performing rights organizations.

Chapter 31
Ring Tones

With the help of the internet mobile music may save the music industry. Ring tones are becoming the new singles. If a major artist like Mariah Carrie song clip is 1.99 per download it would only take a few months for it to make millions. By the time the album hit number 5 on the Billboard the possibility of the ring tone going platinum is not so impossible.

Just like everything else, be sure to keep an eye on the money you can make with ring tones.

Chapter 32
Jingles

There are two types of songs used for jingles, there's the one written specifically for an advertising campaign, and the one using an existing song. If you are interested in having your song used in advertisements you would need to be with an advertising agency or an advertising music provider such as jingle house.

The amount that is normally charged by a music supplier who is writing for a specific advertisement ranges from $7,500 to as much as $25,000 for one 30 second commercial, unless it involves a major celebrity, in this case the cost can be millions. In the case of an existing song for a national commercial, the rate an advertiser must pay to obtain a master use license and sync license of a popular song can run anywhere from $50,000 to over 1,000,000.

Chapter 33
Be In The Know

Because the industry is constantly changing, as an artist you need to be abreast of what's new in the industry. It is your responsibility to invest into your career. Read books pertaining to your specific art form, go to seminars that gears to anyone wanting to get into the industry, like the one 105 FM held 2005 in New York, it was a very informative music seminar with industry heads giving advice. Also Gwendolyn Quinn writers seminar is held at least 2-3 times a year. If you cannot wait for the next seminar another resource would be themusicip.com, where a number of information could be obtained. There is information everywhere you just have to look.

Chapter 34
Sign or Not To Sign

I must stress when it comes to signing contracts, read it yourself first and if you don't understand it then proceed to getting your lawyer to read and explain it. The bottom line is, if you don't understand it don't sign it. Also if you don't agree with things in the contract ask to have it revised, remember **there is no such thing as a standard contract.** In fact a contract is an agreement between two or more entities, agreement being the operative word.

Chapter 35
Use What You Have

God approached Moses in the wilderness through the burning fiery bush and told him to return to Egypt, confront Pharaoh, and lead the Hebrews up from slavery. Moses immediately said I don't have what it takes.

So God says to Moses, What is that in your hand? (Exodus 4:2) Moses replied, Well, Lord, all I have is this shepherd's staff, and God says, That will do.

This is what you need to know, if you consider yourself an artist you need to show your art. You have to eat, sleep, live your art, every where you go and everyone you meet need to know what your art is without asking, so sing in the supermarket, enter talent shows, make-up your own talent show and

100 invite neighbors and friends. Use what you have right now. Make flyers in black and white until you can afford color. When Destinys Child began, they performed every time they got a chance; you can do the same also.

Chapter 36
Know Your Fans

It's becoming increasingly more difficult for companies to treat consumers as one group with one need. The focus now is to individualize whereas making a more accurate connection where consumers unique needs are all round Whether it is the iPod, satellite radio services such as XM, Web sites, the availability of live music performances on AOL, music videos streaming off Launch.com or the self-tailored satisfaction of burning a homemade mix on CD, fans are your chief asset going forward, it is in your best interest as an artist to know the people that want to really know you. The more you know about your fans the more you can give back to them. Involve them, empower them, mobilize them, let them co-create with you. Provide potential customers with as much choice as possible. Learn the technologies that will help you customize your communications with customers and fans.

You should be figuring out how to distribute your work through digital music services now. The Net is your Open Mic to the world. As the industry moves away from physical product, it becomes increasingly important for musicians to learn the rules of licensing. Seek out users of music as well as buyers. Develop marketing plans for both your selected singles as well as for your full-length albums. 50% of current online music sales are in the singles format.

Chapter 37
Next Music Generation

The appetite for music only grows around the globe and you can satisfy it. You'll need to take fuller responsibility for your own success, and beware of standard industry practices that can chain your career. It's time to think outside the normal channels of business and imagine new kinds of companies. Creative partnerships are the key. Combining good music, cheap, global distribution and business savvy almost guarantees success in this world which craves music.

Chapter 38
Music Market

Since few of us have the time, money or energy to mount national marketing campaigns, it is in our best interest to discover and concentrate on a niche, a segment that we can explore towards successful enterprise. Find your niche. Whatever it is it will meet at the crossroads where your most compelling desires intersect with your background resources and current opportunities.

Chapter 39
Small Things

The best thing in the world is NOT a record deal; it is waking up to your own ideas and decision. If you feel like it, start your own company and release your music through it.

Chapter 40
Plan Your Business

No one needs to tell you how much it costs to launch a successful music career. Between equipment, insurance, taxes, travel, recording, mixing, manufacturing, promotion, advertising and various fees and commissions, there is not much left to call your own. Investors are willing to put up a certain amount of dollars to launch your music project with the hope and expectation of a return on their investment.

A plan reflects professional responsibility to the lending institution and greatly increases your chances of securing a loan. A well put together plan will give way for clear creative thinking, it will pinpoint strengths and weaknesses, identify obstacles and problems, expose hidden opportunities, set proper priorities, coordinate your marketing program, take the guesswork out of budgeting and allow for meaningful review and revision.

Chapter 41
Self Distribution

Send a sample of your product. Most distributors accept finished product for consideration only. If you are pressing your own CDs and selling them, in distributors eyes, you are a label. A label must have its own name, catalog numbers, and Universal Product Code. We recommend a trademark search when naming your company. When designing the packaging, the catalog number should be clearly visible on the spines. The catalog number should be the same for CD and Cassette. The UPC Code Bar Code) must be on the back cover of the CD and Cassette. Most distributors cannot distribute any product that is not bar coded.

Chapter 42
Promote Yourself

Your publicity tools will include creative promotional materials like photos, tapes/CDs, press kits, press releases and novelties. Each of these could fill a separate article. For now I will simply list them with their most relevant features.

These include your primary graphic ambassadors-- name, logo, letterhead, envelopes, business cards, mailing labels, flyers, etc. Remember: You never get a second chance to make a first impression so go for the highest quality affordable. When designing your material, think unity: of color, tone, line and texture. Use your logo prominently on all your pieces. This enhances your image and instills top-of-the-mind awareness.

You can get a lot of publicity out of a good

photograph. 8x10 B&W glossies are the standard. Have some 5x7 color shots available too. This will maximize your exposure possibilities. The 8x10s should have the artists logo/name at the bottom along with current contact information. Soloists should have both head shots and full body shots. When doing a photo shoot count on going through at least three rolls of film. If you get one or two useable pictures from each roll you're doing fine. It's also a good idea to have a number of 5x7 action shots of you performing at a high-profile event, receiving an award, or any other scene that's worthy of notice. Use a professional photographer if at all possible. Check local art schools for students who want to earn a few extra dollars. A CD undeniably lends your act more credibility. However less than seventy percent of American households and offices have CD players while over 90% have cassette players. For demo purposes a high-quality cassette with 3 or 4 good songs is all you need. For more general marketing of your act, or when you're intent is to impress, either a full-length cassette or CD is the best choice. In all cases the music should be of the highest production quality affordable and the packaging consonant with all the other publicity materials. Be sure to include your name and contact number on all items! You'd be surprised how often press kit materials become separated.

You send a press release, also called news release. It's a standard tool that works better than letters and phone calls. It's universally used to publicize people and events. The release is essentially a pared-down news story that presents the outline of your event in a way that will grab an editors attention.

Anything newsworthy should be in the news. Special upcoming shows; formation of a new band; record release parties; production of a video; signing a management, agent, distribution, publishing or recording deal; recitals; involvement in a benefit; winning a songwriting contest. These are just a few of the events worthy of mention. Always type and double-space the artists information preferably on their own letterhead. At the top write **FOR IMMEDIATE RELEASE** and then send it off to everyone on your media list.

Short of obtaining professional help, most musicians and songwriters are going to have to go it alone for a time

Start by asking for local recommendations. Also notice which bands and musicians are getting a lot of quality press coverage. Call the publication and ask who the artists publicist is. Publicists specializing in music will often advertise in music magazines. Shop around. Never take the first person who's available. You have nothing with which to compare his or her skills. Prices vary and so does creativity.

Once you've found several possibilities use the following guidelines to be sure you get exactly what you need. Consider: The individual or firm should be inventive, they should be able to create distinction and dimension, the individual or firm should be interested in what you're doing, the individual or firm should not be over loaded with other clients whereas they cannot pay much attention to your needs, be sure to know if the firm or individual is servicing any of your competition and don't forget to find out cost.

It's completely reasonable to request samples of their work and client references. Understanding how the media works is not merely a matter of idle curiosity. Whether you're a band, a soloist, a personal manager, booking agent or other music professional, having access to the media on a continuing, positive basis is a decided advantage.

Chapter 43
Big Deal

Piracy

Unsigned artist, you may not think piracy is such a big deal now, but remember what goes around, comes around and if you ever get signed to a label producing mass amounts of hit records you may also acquire mass amounts of piracy, then, and only then you will understand why it is such a BIG DEAL. Now is the time for you as an aspiring artist to take a stand against piracy whereas the people who know you now will know that you were always against the stealing of another persons chance to live and provide for their family, which is why we all work.

Attorney Selection

Unless a lawyer regularly deals with management, recording, and music publishing contracts; copyright protection and administration; and licensing of intellectual and artistic property, chances are he or she won't sufficiently understand or appreciate the industry and it's peculiar problems.

Always ask the attorney for at least two client-references you can call. This is a perfectly reasonable request.

Ask the attorney about his/her basic philosophy of life. Because this will help you understand his/her worldview, a significant relationship component. If your worldview turns out to be diametrically opposed to the attorneys, it probably means you're not a good match for each other. Inquire about the extent and quality of the attorneys industry contacts; find out how the fee structure would work to avoid any misunderstandings.

Sometimes you'll need legal counsel for short-term projects like putting together the appropriate performance and partnership agreements, trade marking your business/band name, incorporating your business, and copyright registration. These kinds of projects are usually paid for as a flat fee based on the attorneys hourly rate.

Longer-term, projects and legal representation to the music industry are often paid in points (percentage points) of contract advances and/or future royalties.

Chapter 44
Perform, Perform, Performance

Normally, development companies and your manager may be the ones to seek out showcases and other events whereas you can show off your talent.

It being your talent, it is also your responsibility to seek out opportunities to perform.

All your performances does not have to be at Carnegie Hall, you can start right in church, school, or like Destinys child, some times the supermarket will have to do. The truth is; it is your job to be on the job even when you're not on the job.

Let your manager do what he or she does, let the development company do what they do and you do what you do best.

Reading Suggestions

The Music Business by David Naggar

All you need to know about the Music Business by Donald Passam

How to Write a Hit song by Molly-Ann Leikin

Start and Run Your Own record label by Daylle, Deanna, Schwartz

Making Music Make Money – Eric, Beall, Susan, Gedutus, Lindsay (Editor), Berklee Press (Manufactured by)

Music Money and Success by Jeffrey, Brabec, Todd, Brabec

Bibliography

Books:

Naggar, David Esq. The Music Business
   San Francisco: Daje Publishing, 2000
   http://www.ascap.com/filmtv/movies-part2.html
   (Sep, 2006)

WWW:

Jeffrey Brabec and Todd Brabec, "Music, Money,
   Success and the Movies" 2001
   http://www.ascap.com/filmtv/movies-part2.html
   (ep, 2006)

Encyclopedia:

"History of Music"
   Wikipedia The Free Encyclopedia.

Printed in the United States
113962LV00001BB/4/A

9 781432 705817